I0823123

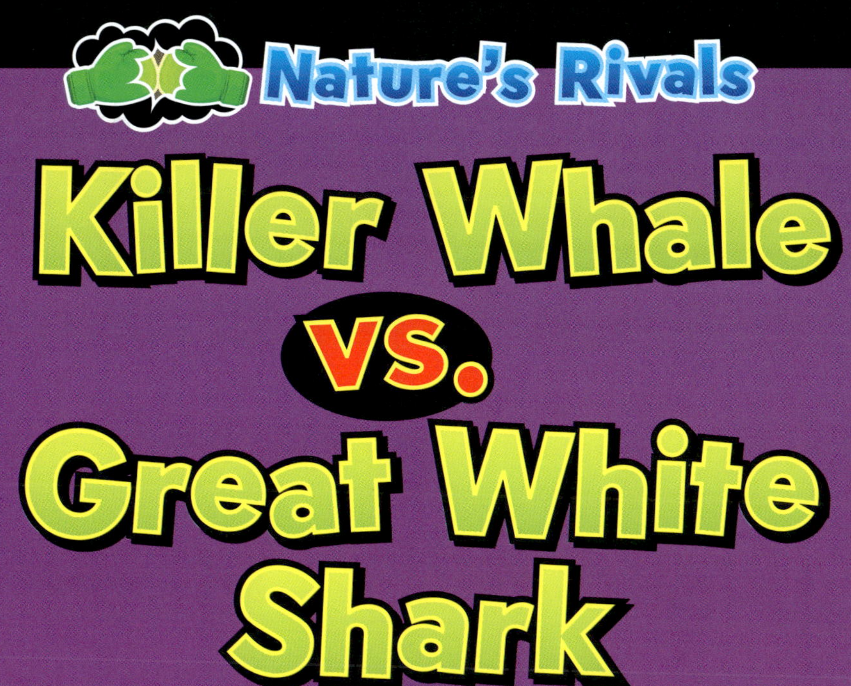

Killer Whale vs. Great White Shark

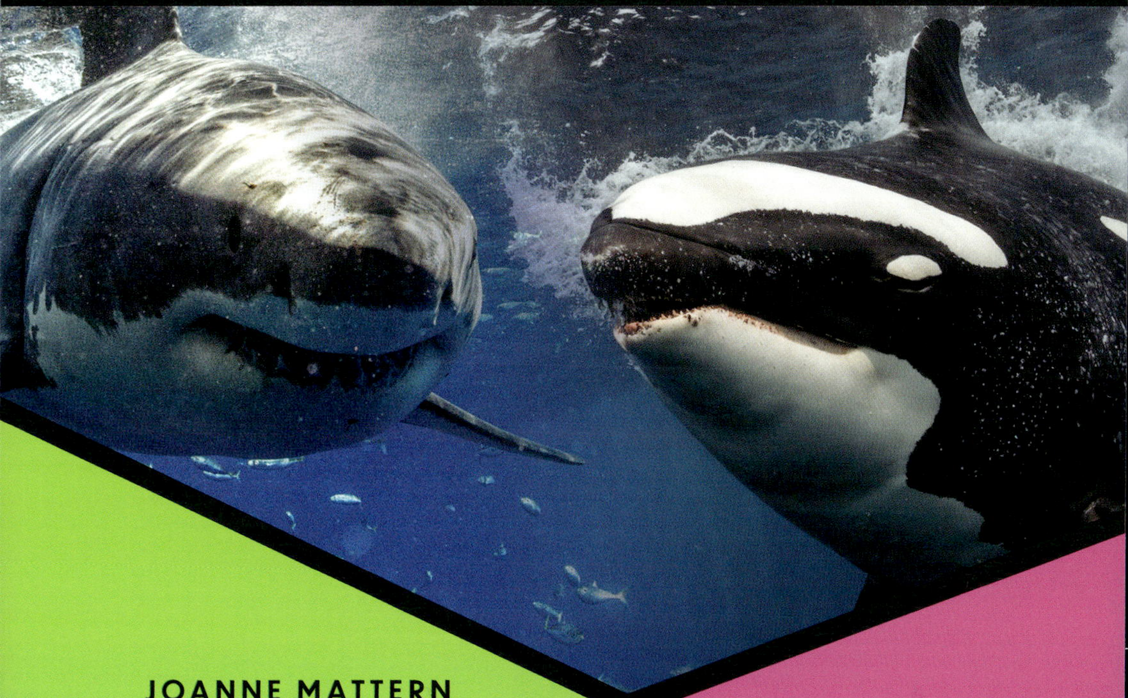

JOANNE MATTERN

Mitchell Lane
PUBLISHERS

Parent and Caregiver Tips for Creating Nonfiction Readers

The high-interest topics in the *Nature's Rivals* series are sure to get your young reader excited about reading nonfiction. While exploring a fascinating subject, your reader will be introduced to new concepts, facts, ideas, and vocabulary.

Tips for Reading Nonfiction

Talk about Nonfiction

Explain that nonfiction books provide facts about real-world topics. When readers read nonfiction, they gain a rich understanding of the world. They build background knowledge that provides a foundation for learning and academic success.

Look at the Parts

This book contains the following helpful features. Share the purpose of each feature with your reader.

Photos, Captions, and Graphic Aids
The photos, captions, charts, maps, and other graphic aids in nonfiction texts contain a wealth of information. Help your reader identify different ways information can be displayed.

Sidebars
These extra tidbits of information help satisfy readers' curiosity and expand their knowledge.

Table of Contents
Located at the front of the book, this list shows the big ideas within the text and the page numbers where they can be found.

Glossary
Located at the back of the book, the glossary defines key words and phrases that are related to the topic. These words and phrases can be found in the text in **bold** type.

Comprehension Questions (Fact Check)
Multiple-choice questions help readers self-check to make sure they understand what they read.

Index
Located at the back of the book, the index is an alphabetical list of topics and the page numbers where they can be found.

With a little help and guidance, your reader will be on their way to enjoying and learning from nonfiction books.

Mitchell Lane
PUBLISHERS
mitchelllanepub.com

2001 SW 31st Avenue
Hallandale, FL 33009

First Edition, 2026.
Author: Joanne Mattern
Designer: Jen Bowers
Editor: Tricia Hoffman

Series: Nature's Rivals
Title: Killer Whale vs. Great White Shark / by Joanne Mattern

Hallandale, FL : Mitchell Lane Publishers, [2026]

Library bound ISBN: 979-8-89260-602-8
Paperback ISBN: 979-8-89260-614-1
eBook ISBN: 979-8-89260-607-3

PHOTO CREDITS
Alamy: John Simmons, 21; Shutterstock: Shane Myers Photography, cover and 1, 8, Ansarphotographer, cover and 1, 7; Wirestock Creators, 3; George R Hughes, 4, Sergey Uryadnikov, 4; wildestanimal, 5; Kertu, 6; USMANboy, 7, 28; Martin Prochazkacz, 9; Willyam Bradberry, 10; Mayskyphoto, 11, iqbaldesigner, 11; Guillermo El OsO, 12; Foto 4440, 13, 25; MuhammadHanif1, 14, 28; Tatiana Ivkovich, 15; karelnoppe, 16, slowmotiongli, 16; Sergey Uryadnikov, 17; Alessandro De Maddalena, 18, 27; Andrea Izzotti, 19; Sergey Uryadnikov, 20, 22; Wirestock Images, 23; LuckyStep, 24; Love Lego, 26; bigjom jom, 27; Peter Hermes Furian, 28

Contents

Battle Under the Sea 4

A Killer Creature 10

A Scary Predator 16

The Ocean Battle Continues . . . 22

Killer Whale vs. Great White Shark 28

Glossary 30

Fact Check 31

Further Reading 31

Index 32

About the Author 32

Battle Under the Sea

A dark shape moves through the ocean. It's a great white shark looking for food. Her **dorsal fin** cuts through the water as she hunts.

A group of sea lions is swimming in the water. The shark can smell them. It looks like dinner is near. She moves in to attack.

But the shark is not the only **predator** nearby! Huge, dark shapes move through the waves. A **pod** of killer whales is on the hunt. And they are ready to fight the great white shark for her meal. A big, bloody battle is about to go down.

The shark sees the killer whales coming closer. She swims fast and rams into the closest killer whale. Her strong jaws take a big bite out of the animal's side. The killer whale's flesh rips and tears. Blood stains the water.

The other killer whales come to help their friend. The shark chomps down, taking another bite with her sharp teeth. But then, one of the killer whales slams his tail down on the shark. The shark starts to sink. What will happen next?

At Home Anywhere

Both killer whales and great white sharks live in oceans all over the world.

A Killer Creature

Killer whales are also called orcas. That is actually a better name for this creature. Why? Because orcas aren't whales at all.

These huge creatures are the largest members of the dolphin family. Males can be up to 32 feet (9.7 meters) long. They weigh between 8,000 and 12,000 pounds (3,629 and 5,443 kg).

Not a Fish

Although killer whales live in water, they are not fish. Like other dolphins, these creatures are **mammals**.

Killer whales have huge jaws. These jaws are filled with about 50 big, sharp teeth. Each tooth measures about four inches (10 cm) long, or about the length of three large paperclips. That makes for one big bite!

These creatures are **carnivores**. They eat seals, sea lions, penguins, and fish. They even eat other whales. The killer whale has no enemies except people.

Smart Creatures

Killer whales have big brains. They are very smart animals.

Killer whales live in big groups. As many as 50 killer whales live in one pod. Killer whales work together. They help each other raise their calves. They hunt **prey** by surrounding it.

These animals hunt by using **echolocation**. They make clicking sounds. The sound waves spread out through the water. If they hit a fish or other object, the sounds waves bounce back to the killer whale. Now, the whale knows where the fish is ... and it knows just where to hunt.

A Big Appetite

A killer whale can eat up to 500 pounds (227 kg) of food a day.

A Scary Predator

Few animals are as scary as the great white shark. These monsters are about 21 feet (6.4 meters) long. They weigh up to 5,000 pounds (2,268 kg). Females are larger than males.

Sharks are built for hunting. Sharks' bodies can move quickly through the water. Their strong tails help them swim fast to catch their prey. These sharks eat seals, sea lions, dolphins, and turtles.

A shark's body has no bones. Instead, it is made of a tough, stretchy material called **cartilage**. Cartilage is a lot lighter than bone. That makes it easier for the shark to swim fast.

Great white sharks have some of the most powerful jaws of any animal. These jaws are filled with about 300 teeth set in rows. When a tooth falls out or breaks, another tooth moves in to take its place. Sharks' teeth have sharp edges that can cut and tear flesh and bone.

Sharks also have a great sense of smell. They can smell a single drop of blood in the water. They can smell when an animal is nearby. Sharks have good eyesight too. It's no wonder these animals are some of the fiercest predators in the ocean!

Unlike other fish, great white sharks are warm-blooded. Being warm-blooded gives them more energy. And more energy means better hunting skills!

Sometimes two sharks will hunt together. But most of the time, these sharks are solitary creatures. They like to be alone.

Swimmers Beware!

Although shark attacks are rare, some great white sharks have attacked people.

The Ocean Battle Continues

Usually, great white sharks swim in colder water than killer whales do. But sometimes they hunt in the same place. That's what happened to the great white shark we met earlier in the book. Let's see what's happening with that fierce ocean battle!

Life at the Top

Both killer whales and great white sharks are **apex predators**. They are at the top of the food chain.

The great white shark was sinking underwater. But now, she is swimming back to the killer whales. Her powerful jaws open wide to attack. But the killer whales are ready for her. They make a circle around the shark.

A few of the killer whales ram the shark. They bite the shark again and again. The shark tries to fight back.

The great white shark chomps down on a killer whale's tail. But another killer whale rams the shark. He flips the shark over onto her back. The shark tries to flip over before another killer whale comes in for the kill.

What will happen next? Think about each animal's weapons and defenses. Then, you decide! Who do you think will win this epic ocean battle?

Killer Whale vs. Great White Shark

Range of Killer Whale

Range of Great White Shark

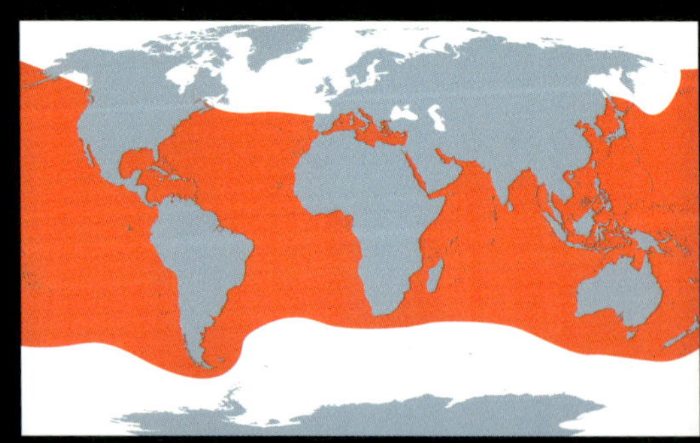

Let's Compare

Killer Whale: Weight—8,000 to 12,000 pounds (3,629 to 5,443 kg); Length—up to 32 feet (9.7 meters)

Great White Shark: Weight—up to 5,000 pounds (2,268 kg); Length—up to 21 feet (6.4 meters)

Killer Whale: About 50 long, sharp teeth

Great White Shark: About 300 jagged teeth

Killer Whale: Powerful bite, sharp teeth, strong tail, hunts in groups, fast swimmer

Great White Shark: Sharp teeth, powerful jaws, fast swimmer, warm-blooded

Killer Whale: Swims fast, attacks in groups

Great White Shark: Powerful jaws and teeth, swims fast

apex predators (AY-peks PRED-uh-turz)
animals that are too big and strong to be eaten by other animals

carnivores (KAHR-nuh-vorz)
animals that only eat meat

cartilage (KAHR-tuh-lij)
strong, elastic tissue found in the body

dorsal fin (DOR-sl fin)
a flat, thin body part located on a shark's back

echolocation (ek-oh-loh-KAY-shun)
finding objects by bouncing sound waves off of them

mammals (MAM-uhlz)
animals that are warm-blooded, have hair or fur, and nurse their babies

pod (PAHD)
a large group of killer whales

predator (PRED-uh-tur)
an animal that eats other animals

prey (PRAY)
an animal that is hunted by another animal for food

Fact Check

1. Killer whales live in groups called _______.
   A. colonies B. schools C. pods

2. Killer whales hunt by using _______.
   A. sound waves B. their eyesight C. their sense of touch

3. A shark's body has no _______.
   A. teeth B. bones C. cartilage

4. Great white sharks and killer whales live _______.
   A. all over the world B. in warm places C. in just one ocean

Answers
1. C, 2. A, 3. B, 4. A

BOOKS

Adamson, Thomas. *Great White Shark vs. Killer Whale*. Bellwether Media, 2020.

Klepinger, Teresa. *Great White Shark vs. Killer Whale*. Kaleidoscope, 2022.

Markle, Sandra. *On the Hunt with Great White Sharks*. Lerner Publications, 2022.

ON THE INTERNET

Britannica Kids: Killer Whale
kids.britannica.com/students/article/killer-whale/576927
This article includes interesting facts about killer whales, including what they eat, where they live, and how they behave.

National Geographic Kids: Killer Whale Facts!
www.natgeokids.com/uk/discover/animals/sea-life/killer-whale-facts/
Learn all about these giant sea creatures at this fact-filled site.

National Geographic Kids: Great White Shark
kids.nationalgeographic.com/animals/fish/facts/great-white-shark
Learn fun facts and view videos and pictures about these killer creatures of the ocean.

Index

blood 8, 19, 20, 29

diet 13, 15, 17

echolocation 15

great white shark 4–9, 16–29

killer whale 4–15, 22–29

orca 10

tail 9, 17, 26, 29

teeth 9, 12, 18, 29

About the Author

Joanne Mattern has written many nonfiction books for children. Whales and sharks are some of her favorite animals, even though she thinks they are pretty scary! Since she doesn't live near a beach, she has never seen either a shark or a whale in the wild, but she hopes to get a look someday. Joanne lives in New York State with her family.